Al Capone

American Gangster Stories

Roger Harrington

Table of Contents

Humble Beginnings

Although he ultimately became notorious as a crime boss engaged in bootlegging, gambling and various other illegal activities and was named by the Chicago Crime Commission as 'Public Enemy Number 1', Al Capone's beginnings were decidedly humble.

Alphonse Gabriel Capone was born on 17th January 1899 in Brooklyn, New York City. Although many people turn to crime to escape their poor background, this wasn't really the case with Al Capone. His parents were respectable people who emigrated from Italy to Austria-Hungary (now Croatia) in 1893 and then by ship to the U.S.

Father Gabriele was employed as a barber while mother Teresa worked for some time as a seamstress. When they arrived in America, they already had two sons and Teresa was pregnant with a third child. They lived initially in a squalid tenement building near the Navy Yard, a generally rough and noisy area although the family managed to remain normal and law-abiding.

Al Capone was born the fourth of nine children, one of whom died at the age of one. Two brothers, Rafaela James (known as 'Ralph') and Salvatore (or 'Frank'), eventually joined Al in his criminal activities. Ironically, given Capone's later career, one brother — Vincenzo, who changed his name to Richard Hart — became a prohibition agent.

Unhappy Schooldays

Capone attended a strict Catholic school where he struggled with the rules and the brutality he faced there. Despite this, he was a promising pupil at least at first. This all changed, however, when he was expelled at the age of fourteen for hitting a female teacher in the face.

The boy's formal education ended at this point and his descent into a criminal career had begun. The transition was no doubt also helped by the family's move, when he was aged eleven, to Park Slope in Brooklyn. This was a much more ethnically mixed area of New York and it resulted in Capone being affected by wider cultural influences.

Included among those influences was Capone's membership of several local gangs. He initially joined the Junior Forty Thieves and then moved on to the Bowery Boys, the Brooklyn Rippers, James Street Boys Gang and eventually the powerful Five Points Gang in Lower Manhattan. The latter was run by gangster Johnny Torrio, who was to have a huge influence on Capone's life.

Early Career

After being expelled from school, Capone took on various odd jobs in the Brooklyn area, including working in a bowling alley and a candy store. Full-time work followed, primarily at the Harvard Inn on Coney Island, owned by mobster Frankie Yale, where Capone worked as a bartender and bouncer.

Whilst working there, Capone inadvertently insulted a woman patron, resulting in her brother, Frank Gallucio, slashing him across the face with a knife in retribution. This caused three prominent scars on the left side of his face that resulted in the press nicknaming him 'Scarface'. After that, Capone always tried to present the other side of his face to cameras and described his scars as 'war wounds', despite never serving in the military.

On Frankie Yale's insistence, Capone apologised to Gallucio for insulting his sister. Nevertheless, he appeared not to bear a grudge since he later hired Gallucio as his bodyguard.

Becoming a Married Man

On 30th December 1918, aged only nineteen, Capone married Irish Catholic Mae Josephine Coughlin. Since he was under 21 at the time, he required the written permission of his parents before the wedding could go ahead. The couple remained married until his death and had one child,

Albert Francis 'Sonny' Capone, who was born just prior to their marriage.

The marriage appeared to change Capone, if only temporarily, and he reportedly worked for a period as a bookkeeper. Within little more than a year, however, he was off to Chicago to work for old associate Johnny Torrio and his career as a criminal really took off.

Moving On

The reasons for Capone's move to Chicago from New York in 1920 are somewhat unclear. There is a belief that the unexpected death of his father prompted a change while there were stories that there was a need to get out after severely injuring a rival gang member. More likely is that he went at the request of Johnny Torrio, for whom he'd worked when aged only fifteen, since he immediately became employed by him on arriving there.

At the time, Torrio operated as an enforcer for crime boss James 'Big Jim' Colosimo. When Colosimo was murdered on 11th May 1920, with the culprits rumored to be either

Capone or Frankie Yale, Torrio took over the business.

Capone initially worked as a bouncer in a brothel. Here he contracted syphilis, which went untreated because the symptoms subsided and he wrongly assumed the disease had somehow been cured. It returned with a vengeance later and was to eventually lead to the deterioration in his physical and mental health that ultimately contributed to his early death.

Opportunities Abound

The start of the Prohibition era in 1920 offered great opportunities to make immense amounts of money from illegal bootlegging operations. And Chicago was ideally located to capitalize on these opportunities, being well served by railroads and with easy access to huge areas of the USA and Canada.

Added to that, Chicago was a city that had grown from a mere 30,000 people in 1850 to around three million when Capone arrived. The influx of all types and nationalities provided a ready market for what he was supplying.

Although Colosimo had been active in operating many brothels and gambling dens in the city, he had supposedly wanted nothing to do with bootlegging. Torrio, however, had no such qualms and, on taking over, went into bootlegging in a big way.

Capone's business sense led to him taking over the running of the Four Deuces, a whorehouse, speakeasy and gambling joint that was also Torrio's headquarters. The basement area was reputedly used to torture opponents and those with useful information. Capone soon became Torrio's right-hand man, helping to run the biggest organised crime group in Chicago.

Torrio had a reputation as a 'gentleman gangster' and his style was to avoid conflict with rival gangs, instead preferring to negotiate with them over territory agreements. These attempts failed in the case of Dean O'Banion, the leader of the smaller North Side Gang, whose territory was increasingly threatened by the Genna brothers and apparently with Torrio's blessing.

On Torrio's orders or agreement, O'Banion was murdered on 24th October 1924. O'Banion's close friend Hymie Weiss took over the North Side Gang and made revenge over the killing a priority. That resulted in an unsuccessful attempt on Capone's life in January 1925 and Torrio being shot multiple times twelve days later.

Capone's Ascension to Gang Boss

Although Torrio recovered from his injuries, he retired and handed over full control to Capone. He returned to his native Italy for a period of three years before eventually coming back to the US.

At the age of 26, Al Capone was in charge of an organization, which he referred to as the 'Outfit' that included gambling, prostitution and illegal breweries backed up by a transport network that spread across America and into Canada.

All of that came with protection from law enforcement agencies and politicians, together with a degree of ignorance — some newspapers describing him as a 'boxing promoter' due to him having promoted local fights in order to raise extra money. Capone marked his elevation by increasing the organization's revenue through the use of uncompromising tactics.

Any businesses that refused to deal with him were treated harshly. That generally meant their property being blown up, around one hundred people losing their lives during the 1920s to these bombings.

Capone's hardline approach meant that the power vacuum usually associated with a gang boss's demise never happened. He quickly smashed all the opposition that would otherwise have been fighting for control and established a supremacy that few dared threaten.

In the event, the outcome was a significant increase in brothels and a business that generated revenue of as much as $100 million annually, equivalent to around $1.2 billion today. Capone had in place a network of brothels and speakeasies throughout the city and controlled the sale of alcohol to more than 10,000 speakeasies. By 1929, his personal net worth had risen to over $40 million — a figure that equates to about $550 million at today's values.

Gaining Influence

In order to gain the protection of Chicago city hall for his bootlegging operations, Capone is widely believed to have helped Republican William Hale Thompson gain election as mayor. By 1923, having put up with the corruption of Thompson as well as his alliance with Torrio for eight years, Chicago elected reformer William Dever as his successor. Fearing a crackdown on his operations, Torrio decided a second base was needed and sent Capone to nearby Cicero to establish a presence there.

Building a Political Base

The potential crackdown on racketeering in Chicago brought into focus the importance of increasing protection against the law enforcement agencies. That objective was largely achieved by a combination of bribery and strong-arm tactics.

To protect their gambling dens, brothels and other illegal activities, Capone and Brothers Frank and Ralph attained leading positions in the Cicero city government. This was partly achieved by threatening voters and kidnapping the election workers of their opponents, although Frank was killed in a Chicago police shoot out during this period.

Capone used threats, bribery and violence to move existing gangster gangs aside. This caused a change in political opinion and existing mayor Joseph Klenha, who was up for re-election in April 1924, asked Capone for help. He responded by turning gang members loose on the election.

Klenha's opponent was forced out of his headquarters by gunmen, the challenger for the city clerk's office was pistol whipped and helpers and campaigners were beaten up. Election workers were kidnapped, policemen attacked and voters who were planning to support the opposition were prevented from voting.

The whole election fell into chaos and officials asked for help. As a result, seventy Chicago police officers were deputised and five squads of detectives were sent to Cicero to restore order.

One squad came across three gunmen who included Al and Frank Capone. In the shoot-out that followed, Frank was killed and Al managed to escape unharmed. In common with many such episodes over several years, he was not arrested.

The campaign of violence was effective, however, since Klenha was comfortably re-elected. With Klenha in his pocket, Capone established his headquarters in the Hawthorne Inn and took over the town.

Klenha was again elected in 1928, although this time there was no repeat of the violence due to a large Chicago police presence. By 1932, the electorate had had enough and Klenha was voted out. Capone, however, wasn't overly concerned since by this time he was already serving time for tax evasion.

Back in Chicago, in the 1927 election, Thompson won the backing of Capone, allegedly to the extent of a $250,000 contribution, by campaigning for a wide open city that might even include the re-opening of illegal saloons.

Thompson won by a narrow margin in 1927, helped by a bombing campaign on the 10th April polling day that targeted booths in areas that were thought to support Thompson's rival William Emmett Dever. Also a victim was lawyer Octavius Granadary, who challenged Thompson's candidature for the African-American vote and was shot and killed after being chased through the streets by cars containing armed men.

Capone's bomber, James Belcastro, was charged along with four police officers but all charges were subsequently dropped when witnesses retracted their statements.

Maintaining Authority and Security

For a period, Capone moved his Chicago headquarters to fifty rooms within the luxurious Metropole Hotel. This was a statement of his authority in the knowledge that Mayor Thompson would comply with his wishes. That authority extended to his mobsters carrying official police department issue cards stating that the bearer should be treated with the same courtesy as police officers.

Whilst the actions in connection with the elections served to safeguard Capone's operations, his life was still in danger. Despite this, he was generally unarmed but was always accompanied by a minimum of two bodyguards and even acquired an armor plated car for his protection. He rarely risked travelling during the day, preferring night-time travel as a safer option.

There was also a tendency to get away from Chicago at every opportunity. This often included taking a night train to various cities, booking at the last minute an entire carriage for Capone and his entourage. On arrival at their destination, they'd book into a luxury hotel under assumed names, occupying suites for up to a week.

Creating his Miami Beach Base

In 1928, Capone bought a 14-room house on Palm Island, Florida. It was purchased from beer magnate Clarence Busch for $40,000 and had ten-foot walls behind which Capone could get away from public attention.

It was a place where he could escape Chicago's harsh winters while still being able to direct operations from there, sometimes on the 32-foot cabin cruiser he had acquired. Palm Island was also the place where Capone eventually spent his final days on release from prison.

The purchase of the Florida mansion was partly prompted by a need to break free from the pressures and persecutions of Chicago. It also resulted from a journey between various cities where Capone was greeted at each one by a large police presence and it was made clear he was not welcome there.

Capone liked Florida in general and Miami in particular. This was due to the benign year round weather and the indulgent lifestyle where gambling was everywhere and prohibition was largely ignored.

Planning to establish a base there, he booked into the penthouse suite of the Ponce de Leon Hotel under the name of 'A Costa'. He also rented a house on Miami Beach for his wife and son at a cost of $2,500 per month.

The property was leased under the name of 'Al Brown' as a precaution. Nevertheless, the owners soon found out who the real occupant was and worried about the safety of the building and its contents. Their fears were misplaced because Capone actually upgraded some of the contents to meet his lifestyle needs and ensured all bills related to the property were settled in full.

How the Palm Island Property was Acquired

The Ponce de Leon Hotel was operated by Parker Henderson Junior, who was eager to please and provided favors for Capone, including purchasing a number of guns for him. He also acted as a real estate representative for Capone and helped locate and acquire the Palm Island mansion where he spent his final days.

The mansion was bought on 27th March 1928 but, knowing Capone wouldn't be welcome as a resident, Henderson signed all the papers as though he was the purchaser and owner of the property.

Capone spent $100,000 improving the estate, adding what was at the time the largest privately-owned swimming pool with a filtration system that could handle sea or fresh water. Also added were new garages, a boathouse, decking and gardens. Capone supervised all the work and insisted on the best of everything but, like the house, it was all done in Henderson's name.

To ensure the highest standards of work, Capone treated all his workers well. That included providing them with sumptuous lunches and the result was a renovation project of which he was proud.

It took some time before it was realized who the real owner of the property was. This was despite Henderson transferring the mansion into the name of Mae Capone, Al's wife.

Attempts to Move Capone Out of Florida

Economic events had slowed the property market and a hurricane in 1926 had not helped matters. So it was feared Capone's arrival would make matters worse and turn Miami Beach into a place where people didn't want to come.

Several local groups protested at Capone's presence in Miami, prompting a meeting with the mayor and the Miami Beach city mayor. They appeared satisfied with his explanation that he was there for relaxation and would not cause any trouble.

Although the area was alive with illegal gambling, prostitution and other corrupt activities, to which local officials had turned a blind eye; Capone was accused of bringing in gambling. There was a newspaper-led campaign to get him out and a move by the American League to strip him of his constitutional rights.

The Miami Beach city council tried to sue him while the governor of Florida attempted to have him arrested. This occurred on a few occasions but only resulted in him being jailed once. Constant surveillance failed to curb his activities and endless harassment did not succeed in driving him out. Capone did attempt to improve relationships by hosting a series of goodwill dinners but opinions were too firmly entrenched to change matters much.

Residents campaigned for his removal and various authorities combined with business leaders to support this action. Many of the latter, however, saw Capone's presence as a business opportunity and efforts to move him out failed.

Those attempts included arresting Capone on vagrancy charges in April 1930, a ploy that a Chicago judge repeated in September of the same year. Neither charge succeeded in achieving the desired intent.

Centre of Attention

Although he was undoubtedly a gangster who inflicted pain, suffering and death on many people, Capone didn't really see himself in the same light. He liked to portray himself as a pillar of the community and a benevolent character that helped others, opening soup kitchens during the Depression and making significant donations to numerous charities. That image was, however, the complete opposite of the view of many — particularly the law enforcement agencies.

Well-known for his brutality, Capone was described by the New Yorker in 1928 as 'the greatest gang leader in history'. Against that, he considered himself a gentleman and believed the jobs he provided, criminal though they may be, created an income for people who would otherwise be poor. He liked to be described as some sort of Robin Hood, who gave to the poor at the expense of the rich.

Many people, particularly Italian immigrants, viewed him as a community leader who helped the poor. One of his projects was to provide daily milk to poor Chicago schoolchildren to help prevent rickets. He would send flowers to the funerals of rival gang members and had a reputation for helping people who were in need.

A Sharp Dresser

Capone was a flamboyant character who wore sharp, pin stripe or chalk suits and fedora hats in lighter, contrasting colors, often with a cigar in his mouth, an image on which numerous fictitious gangster characters are based. The suits were in a variety of colors ranging from charcoal through to lighter summer colors, especially when in Florida. The suit lengths were often imported from Italy at a price that was the equivalent of $6,500 each today.

He was generally adorned with gaudy jeweler, which he dispensed with at his trial for tax evasion in order to display a more conservative image. His more human side also extended to a love of fishing, singing and writing music.

Despite his Italian roots and his membership of what was in essence a crime group with a very Italian background, Capone was fiercely American. If at any time he was described as Italian, he would proudly insist that he was born in Brooklyn.

Maintaining a High Profile

He loved his celebrity status and nourished it by always being available to talk to the press. When questioned about his activities, he portrayed himself as a respectable businessman who aimed to satisfy demand and was providing a public service by doing so.

Capone's courting of the press and his quest for publicity were things that later came back to haunt him. In interviews while in prison, he voiced regrets at having spoken so extensively to the press because the high profile that resulted had made him a target and had at the very least accelerated his eventual demise.

As well as associating with the press, Capone attended the opera, ball games and other public events where he generally was greeted with standing ovations and people wishing to shake him by the hand. Numerous attempts to increase his profile included moving the headquarters to the luxurious Metropole Hotel for a time.

For a period of four years, from 1925 to 1929, Capone was the most high profile gangster in the country. He worked hard to cultivate his image as a respectable businessman who cared for the people of Chicago. Throughout that period, however, conflicts between the rival gangs were increasing and the violence was growing, which was at variance with the image Capone strove to promote.

He hated the nickname of 'Scarface' that was given to him by the press, since it didn't fit with the image he wanted to put out. Instead, he preferred close friends' reference to him as 'Snorky', a slang term to describe a sharp dresser, or other criminal associates calling him the 'Big Fellow' or 'Big Al'.

Neither of the latter names referred to his height because, at five foot ten inches, he was little over average height although he was at the very least somewhat corpulent. The reference was more likely to his status as undisputed head of criminal activities in Chicago.

At the height of his fame, around 1927, his notoriety had spread throughout the country and even abroad. Tour buses drove past his headquarters, visitors expected to see him and the police even recruited him to greet a group of Italian aviators on a world tour.

Capone reputedly had a long-held belief that he would have been better selling milk than alcohol since there was a lot less hassle and an enduring demand. He did, in fact, own a dairy farm and sold milk in bottles that were labelled with expiry dates, which is something we accept as a regular occurrence today. Back then, it tied in with his stated wish for all milk sold in Chicago to have expiry dates, resulting from a relative apparently having become ill after drinking old milk and, possibly, simply being part of his wish to be seen as a respectable businessman.

Relationships with his Family

Capone was a devoted family man and tried to keep his home life entirely separate from his criminal activities, an approach advocated by his mentor Johnny Torrio. One theory is that he started or at least escalated his life of crime to provide for his family after his father died when he was only 21. He was devoted to his mother and was in daily contact with her whenever possible.

Although Capone's marriage to Mae endured right through to his death, that doesn't mean he remained faithful to her. His sexual deeds led to his contracting syphilis and he then infected his wife with the disease, never admitting he had contracted it since that would have been an admission of adultery. For the same reason, he never undertook treatment despite suffering flu-like symptoms, rashes and sores as a result of it.

The conflicting views of Al Capone once led to someone describing him as the kind of person who would kiss babies during the day and kill their parents at night while they slept. That probably just about sums up his personality and was reflected in the way he did business, negotiating with a smile on his face but destroying and killing those who refused to do business with him on his terms.

Victims and Events

Throughout Capone's career, a whole string of killings and other unsavory events were linked to his name. He was prone to mood swings and frequent violent outbursts, which with hindsight may have been brought on by the gradually worsening dementia that resulted from his syphilis infection.

According to the Chicago Daily Tribune, 33 people were killed, directly or indirectly, by Capone, while others put the figure as high as 700. The earliest of these killings, on 7th May 1923, was Joe Howard, who attempted to hijack a beer consignment belonging to Johnny Torrio and had attacked Jake 'Greasy Thumb' Guzik, the trusted treasurer and financial expert of the Outfit. There was also suspicion that Capone had been involved in the death of 'Big Jim' Colosimo three years previously.

Removing Rival Gang Leaders

At Torrio's request, Capone was believed to have participated in the killing of North Side Gang leader Dean O'Banion in November 1924. That incident resulted in Torrio being shot in a revenge attack, forcing his retirement and causing Capone's accession to the top job. It also, in October 1926, led to the murder of Earl 'Hymie' Weiss, who succeeded O'Banion as North Street Gang leader and vowed to get Capone.

Weiss was the son of Polish immigrants and had formed the North Side Gang along with

Dean O'Banion and George 'Bugs' Moran. He took over after O'Banion's death and made several attempts on Capone's life in a bid to gain revenge.

There had been a previous attempt on Weiss's life after Capone's driver was tortured and killed. Following that, on 20th September 1926, the North Side Gang made a concerted attempt to murder Capone.

After staging a ploy to draw him to the windows of his Hawthorne Inn headquarters, they then opened fire with machine guns and shotguns. Capone escaped unhurt and, after attempts to call a truce failed, Weiss and a companion were killed and three others injured three weeks later outside the North Side headquarters.

The response was to kidnap and kill the owner of the Hawthorne Inn's restaurant, who was a friend of Capone.

Although no-one was ever charged with Weiss's murder, it was widely thought that Capone's top gunman, Jack McGurn, armed with a machine gun, had been one of the two assailants. Trusted associate Frank Nitti was suspected of being responsible for the planning of the hit.

The Killing of Billy McSwiggin

On 27th April 1926, in an event that became known as the Adonis Club Massacre, Thomas Duffy and James Doherty were killed due to their threats against an attempt by Capone and Frankie Yale to bring large quantities of bootleg whiskey into Chicago.

The killings were undertaken by gunmen armed with machine guns. They drove past in five cars and opened fire as members of a rival gang left the Adonis Club bar.

Caught up in the shooting and also killed was assistant state prosecutor Billy McSwiggin, known as the 'hanging prosecutor'. McSwiggin was well-known for going after bootleggers. He had previously attempted to prosecute Capone for the murder of a rival but without success.

Although Capone was suspected but not arrested due to a lack of evidence, there was a big public outcry. That helped to turn public opinion against him and possibly, to some degree, set in motion events that would eventually lead to his downfall.

After McSwiggin's murder, Capone lay low for almost three months. Eventually, he came out of hiding and presented himself to the police. With insufficient evidence to have any hope of gaining a conviction, they had no option but to let him go, thereby increasing even further his aura of invincibility.

Killing for a Purpose

Capone viewed killing rival gang members as an act of self-defense since he was only doing it to protect his business. Although he rarely took part in the killings himself, there were incidences where he was known or suspected of having taken personal responsibility. One of these occurred on 7th May 1928, when he eliminated three men who had been part of a plot to assassinate him.

Former associates, they were invited to a banquet and plied with food and drink. Lulled into a false sense of security, they were tied to their chairs and then Capone systematically beat them to death with a baseball bat in a scene later replicated in 'The Untouchables' film.

Another dozen killings followed over the next eighteen months. Some of these were to get rid of rivals who were threatening the operation. Others were people who had been brought in to kill Capone, who had a $50,000 bounty put on his head by rival mobsters, while some planned to testify against him or did not support him as required.

Capone was rarely personally involved in the killings but ordered others to carry them out on his behalf. An exception came after an assault on friend and accomplice Jack Guzik, Capone shooting the culprit dead in a bar. An absence of witnesses meant he was never charged with the murder but his reputation grew as a result.

As Chicago became more violent, with drive-by killings increasingly frequent and innocent people caught in the cross-fire, Capone somewhat surprisingly acted as a peacemaker. He succeeded in stopping the killings and violence for around two months by arranging an amnesty between the various gangs. However, this was never likely to last long and normal activities soon resumed with street violence and fighting between the gangs.

The Treachery of Frankie Yale

A big problem was the regular hijacking of Capone's whiskey transports. This was largely blamed on Frankie Yale, Capone's long-time associate who was now seen as a rival having turned against him. This was reportedly after the appointment of Tony Lombardo as president of Unione Sicilana, an organisation that supposedly controlled much of the Italian-American vote and from which Capone's outfit received some of its political protection.

Capone had supported Lombardo's candidacy while Yale had backed Joe Aiello. Once Lombardo took over, Yale disapproved of his actions and received reduced income from the Unione. He decided to recover the shortfall from Capone and, being responsible for the safe passage of Capone's whiskey shipments through New York, he instead began to hijack some of them.

Yale was killed by machine gun fire on 1st July 1928 but not before he had ordered Capone's informant against him to be murdered. A gun used in that murder was subsequently found to be one of those acquired by Parker Henderson Junior for Capone and led to Henderson eventually testifying against Capone at his tax evasion trial

The St. Valentine's Day Massacre

The next and most notorious event of all, the St. Valentine's Day Massacre, occurred on 14th February 1929. The North Side Gang, which was now led by George Clarence 'Bugs' Moran in succession to Vincent Drucci, who had taken over on Hymie Weiss's death and then himself been killed, had long been a problem for Capone.

The violence between the North Side Gang and Torrio's South Side Gang (later to become the Chicago Outfit) really grew when the latter started selling alcohol on the North Side's territory. That ultimately led to the murder of O'Banion outside a flower shop that he owned.

The relationship between Capone and Moran gradually deteriorated, with Moran attacking Capone's premises, hijacking his liquor shipments and killing those associated with him. There were numerous attacks and retaliations, including two attempts on Capone's life by drive-by shootings, a form of attack that Moran made popular.

An attempt on the life of Capone's friend and associate, Jack McGurn, at last prompted some action. The plan was to ambush Bugs Moran at a warehouse and garage that served as the North Side Gang's headquarters. Capone's men kept watch from an apartment across the street and, on the morning of 14th February, signalled that they had seen Moran enter the premises.

Some of Capone's men, in police uniforms and a stolen police car staged a raid on the premises and lined seven men up against a wall without a struggle. They were disarmed and then shot in cold blood with machineguns and shotguns.

Six of the men were killed instantly but one, Frank Gusenberg, was still alive despite having taken fourteen bullets. He made it to the hospital but died shortly afterwards.

The main problem for Capone was that Moran, despite the information given to him, was not among the victims. Having seen the police car pull up outside the warehouse, he had made his getaway before the attack took place. All Capone's further attempts to get Moran failed, the gangster eventually dying of lung cancer while serving the second of two ten-year jail sentences for bank robbery.

Aftermath of the St. Valentine's Day Massacre

The atrocity caused public outrage and prompted intense police activity. Up to that point, people had tolerated Prohibition and the lawlessness that came with it. Most of the associated violence revolved around gangsters shooting other gangsters, with usually no direct effect on the general public.

Although this event was really no different, the scale and brutality of the killing caused uproar. Photographs of the aftermath of the attack showed the outcome with gruesome reality, causing a demand for something to be done. That drove President Herbert

Hoover to resolve to make an example of Capone.

Although Capone was suspected of being behind the killings, he was at his mansion in Florida when they took place and supposedly had a note from his doctor confirming that he was confined to his bed. Nevertheless, it is widely believed that Capone planned the Saint Valentine's Day Massacre from his Florida mansion. McGurn was checked into a distant hotel and there was no evidence of either man's involvement, resulting in no-one ever being convicted of the crimes.

McGurn was staying at the hotel with his then girlfriend, Louise Rolfe, who claimed they had spent the whole day together in bed. Nevertheless, the police charged him with the seven murders and subsequently also charged him with crossing state lines with Rolfe, an offence at the time due to her being an unmarried woman. McGurn prevented her testifying against him by divorcing his wife and marrying Rolfe, resulting in all charges being dropped.

McGurn was later named Public Enemy Number Four at the time Capone was Number One on the list. However, he subsequently became ostracized by Capone's outfit and in 1936 was shot and killed.

The main suspects for that killing were Bugs Moran, as revenge for McGurn's part in the St. Valentine's Day Massacre, or the Chicago Outfit because he knew too much about them. McGurn was buried at Mount Carmel Cemetery in Hillside, Illinois, the same resting place as many other gangsters, including Al Capone.

The public reaction to the St. Valentine's Day Massacre added to the determination to convict Capone and was another contributory factor in his eventual downfall. He was summoned to appear before a grand jury in connection with the massacre but failed to attend, claiming he was unwell.

He was finally, in 1931, charged with contempt of court for that failure to appear and ultimately did receive a one-year jail sentence that he served after completing his time for the tax evasion charges. More crucially, since a federal court issued the contempt citation, the FBI became involved and it was their work that eventually brought about his downfall.

An estimated seven further killings took place over the next eighteen months up to 23rd October 1930 before he was found guilty of tax fraud the following year.

The Quest for Justice

Al Capone ruled by terror and murder for many years and was pursued by the police for numerous crimes without success. It is, therefore, somewhat ironic that he was eventually convicted and jailed for something as comparatively simple and harmless as tax evasion.

How Capone Evaded Justice

He avoided prosecution for a long time by a process of bribery and corruption of police and officials combined with intimidating or eliminating potential witnesses. An estimated $30 million was spent in 1927 on bribes to various people who could protect him in some way.

His own employees or associates were either fiercely loyal to him or were too fearful for their own safety to act against him. Although many people knew of his crimes, hardly any of them were prepared to say anything about them. He was also careful not to be linked with criminal acts, ensured alibis were watertight and had no properties registered in his name.

Capone dealt exclusively in cash, having no bank account in his name and apparently only ever signing one cheque (for a gambling debt), so that no transactions could be traced back to him. Nevertheless, the case against him was building slowly (the one cheque in his name being part of the evidence) and the outcome seemed increasingly inevitable.

Gaining the First Convictions

Public outcry against his activities became so great that, in March 1929, President Herbert Hoover insisted to Secretary of the Treasury Andrew Mellon that Capone must be jailed. That started the process that would eventually lead to him being convicted of tax evasion.

Prior to that, Capone's first conviction for a criminal offence came in May 1929 after he was arrested in Philadelphia for carrying a concealed weapon while on his way back from a meeting of crime bosses in Atlantic City, New Jersey. He was convicted and sentenced, within sixteen hours of his arrest, to one year in jail but was freed in March 1930 for good behavior.

One month later, Capone was named Public Enemy Number 1 by the Chicago Crime Commission when it released its first list of wanted criminals. This didn't help the reputation of a man who wanted to be viewed as a solid citizen and businessman.

The Role of Eliot Ness

Federal agent Eliot Ness has been widely credited with bringing about Capone's downfall. That's largely due to his memoirs, 'The Untouchables', which subsequently gave rise to a successful TV series and film, although it is now accepted that his role was somewhat exaggerated. The responsibility for this is largely accredited to co-author Oscar Fraley, who was the source of many of the 'facts' in the book.

Ness's small team of prohibition agents was labelled 'the Untouchables' because they supposedly could not be bribed. They raided illegal breweries and other illicit operations and were involved in Capone's indictment for prohibition violations when he was arrested after testifying to a grand jury on 27th March 1929.

Indeed, Ness's team was able to assemble a bootlegging indictment against Capone that ran to 5,000 charges. That work went to waste to some degree when the decision was later taken to prosecute on tax evasion charges instead.

Ness did succeed in angering Capone greatly by destroying or seizing millions of dollars' worth of brewing equipment, destroying thousands of gallons of alcohol, closing some large breweries and damaging his bootlegging business by exposing prohibition violations. A lot of the increased activity was undertaken after Capone murdered a friend of Ness.

Ness's Innovative Methods

Ness was at the very least innovative in his methods and beliefs. His squad cars were painted in easily recognizable colors and had two-way radios to make communication easy. He pioneered forensic science, with an emphasis on ballistic tests and soil samples, and made use of wiretapping to gather evidence.

His battle against corruption led to the setting up of teams to investigate the bribery of police officers, the forerunner of today's internal affairs divisions. And his views on alcohol and drug addiction were ahead of his time, believing that they were medical problems rather than being treated as criminal acts, as was then the prevalent thought.

Although Ness was certainly above bribery and corruption, he wasn't quite the saintly figure that was portrayed. Some of the alcohol that was impounded was given away to reporters to encourage them to cover the story and Ness himself was partial to a drink. His later years featured periods of heavy drinking after a spell as Cleveland's director of public safety and a failed attempt in 1947 to become Cleveland's mayor, before his death in 1957 at the age of 55.

Ness's death occurred shortly before 'The Untouchables' book was published Although a lot of the content was fictitious nonsense, the book told a great story and was a huge success. As were, of course, the TV series starring Robert Stack as Ness, which ran for four years from 1959, and the film starring Kevin Costner that grossed $76 million.

The Change of Tactics

One of the reasons that Capone evaded justice for so long was that different agencies were responsible for investigating his various activities and the FBI only became involved latterly. Any prohibition offences, for example, were the responsibility of the Bureau of Prohibition while the killings in the St. Valentine's Day Massacre were not classed as federal offences.

In an attempt to run Capone out of Florida, he was arrested on vagrancy charges in April 1930. In February 1931, he was tried for contempt as a result of him failing to attend a grand jury hearing after feigning illness. He was sentenced to six months in jail but was freed while he appealed the conviction.

This was the first time the FBI became involved in the pursuit of Al Capone, being asked by US Attorneys to find out if his excuse of ill-health was genuine. It proved not to be true since, despite Capone being supposedly bed-ridden at the time while suffering from bronchopneumonia, he was spotted at the race track, on holiday and was even being questioned by local prosecutors during that period. That resulted in him being cited for contempt of court and other charges followed on from there.

Preparing for the Tax Evasion Charge

A lot of the credit for Capone's later conviction for tax evasion goes to Elmer Irey, a United States Treasury Department official who was told by Secretary of the Treasury Andrew Mellon that it was the responsibility of his office to put Capone in jail. He led the Internal Revenue Service's investigative unit that built a case against him. That was only possible due to a change of law in 1927 when the Supreme Court decreed that income tax was due on illegal earnings.

This occurred during a trial against bootlegger Manley Sullivan, who was convicted of failing to file a tax return that showed the profits he made from his criminal businesses. An argument that the Fifth Amendment protected criminals from having to report illegal earnings was rejected by Justice Oliver Wendell Holmes Junior.

This cleared the way for the IRS special investigation unit to appoint Frank J Wilson, their most relentless and aggressive investigator, to investigate Capone. He was to focus on his spending as a means of proving his level of income.

Capone's income was obviously substantial since his net worth was estimated at about $30 million in 1929. Despite this, he had never filed an income tax return.

Capone had long maintained to all who would listen that he was a respectable and successful businessman. The main point he had overlooked, however, was that successful businessmen earn a good income and have to pay their taxes on that income. That was a big hole in Capone's record that the government looked to exploit.

Lavish Spending Was the Key

Capone's income was well hidden due to the lack of a bank account and no record of any assets in his name. Consequently, Wilson's team of five investigators concentrated initially on his extravagant lifestyle and uncovered purchases of Lincoln limousines, gold plated dinner services and jewel studded belt buckles. They also found evidence of the booking of luxury hotel suites, the staging of lavish parties and telephone bills amounting to $39,000.

Such levels of spending could only be possible if there was the income to match it but determining that income was little short of impossible. Although the revenue came from hundreds of sources, there was no obvious documentary evidence and no-one willing to testify against Capone. That was due to a sense of loyalty or, more likely in many cases, a fear of their lives or well-being should they dare to talk.

One who did talk was Eddie O'Hare, an operator of dog racing tracks and patent owner of the mechanical lure used in these events. He provided leads for the investigators but eventually paid with his life when he was shot to death just before Capone was released from prison.

Breakthroughs in the Investigation

The investigation ran for two years and the first real breakthrough, in 1930, was the acquisition of three bound ledgers found in a raid on one of Capone's premises. These ledgers appeared to provide evidence of income from a gambling hall although without conclusive proof that they referred to Capone.

Comparison of handwriting in the ledgers identified the author as Leslie Shumway and, having tracked him down to his Florida home; agents threatened him with a subpoena. Aware of the trouble he was in, with Capone certain to exact retribution if he were to divulge information, Shumway took protection and agreed to talk. He submitted an affidavit where he described the gambling business and admitted he took orders from Capone in relation to it.

Another important witness was Frank Reis, who was named on several cashier cheques that were assumed to be intended for Capone. After spending four days in solitary confinement, he admitted to agents that he was employed by Capone and that the cheques covered profits at his Cicero gambling hall. This evidence was later repeated in testimony to a grand jury.

In the trial that followed in 1931, the ledgers were actually inadmissible due to the statute of limitations. However, Capone's lawyers failed to make the necessary objections, although the ledgers themselves did not prove his control of the business.

Around this time, Capone's Brother Ralph was tried and convicted of tax evasion. He was sentenced to three years in prison and this prompted Al Capone to take action so the same didn't happen to him.

Capone's Crucial Mistake that Led to his Conviction

He instructed his lawyers to regularize his tax situation but, in doing so, gave the authorities the information they needed about his income. Capone was present at a meeting, in April 1930, between his tax attorney Lawrence Mattingly and investigator Frank Wilson when the stated intention was to settle his tax dues.

At that meeting, Capone nevertheless refused to admit the level of his income and grew increasingly irritated as it progressed, eventually issuing a thinly veiled threat against Wilson and his wife. Five months later, on 30th September, Capone's lawyers stated in a letter that he was willing to pay tax on income in a specific number of years.

This letter covered the six years that were in dispute. It offered that he would pay tax on Capone's income in that period, ranging from an admitted $26,000 in 1924 through to $100,000 in each of the years 1928 and 1929.

The government now had the documentary evidence it so badly needed of Capone's large amounts of income over several years. It was a grave mistake on Capone's part and resulted in him being charged in 1931 with tax evasion as well as violations of the Volstead Act (Prohibition).

The charges were backed up by other evidence gathered by Elmer Irey's team, agents having infiltrated Capone's organization at great risk to themselves. One informer was killed before he could testify but the two bookkeepers who had been employed by Capone were put under police protection before charges were brought.

The Charges against Capone

The government initially claimed Capone had a 1924 tax liability of more than $32,000, while still investigating the years 1925 to 1929. The grand jury indicted Capone for the 1924 evasion of income tax two days before the statute of limitations would have prevented this. Further counts covering the years 1925 to 1929 were added two months later.

Ultimately, the grand jury found Capone guilty of 22 counts of tax evasion in the sum of over $200,000. Additionally, he and 68 gang members were charged with 5,000 violations of the Volstead Act but the tax evasion charges were considered to have precedence over these.

These were reckoned to have the far greatest chance of success since many jurors would be likely to drink alcohol and therefore have some sympathy with Capone's activities. However, such approval was unlikely to extend to tax evasion, which was generally a detested offence.

The Plea Bargain that Failed

With doubts over the six-year statute of limitations being upheld by the Supreme Court and fears that witnesses could intimidated, US Attorney George E Q Johnson arranged a plea bargain that could see Capone being jailed for as little as two years and no more than five years.

Judge James Herbert Wilkerson, however, would have none of this and refused to allow the deal, so Capone withdrew his guilty plea. Wilkerson was keen to stress that there would be no bargaining with the Federal Government and that the parties involved in a criminal case could not determine the judgment.

How Jury Intimidation was Avoided

Instead, the trial went ahead and a vital element was Judge Wilkerson changing the jury for a fresh one at the last minute and sequestering them each night to prevent them being bribed or intimidated. The action came after the Judge learned that Capone's organization had managed to obtain a full list of all the prospective jurors and was engaged in giving out bribes and making threats to get them on his side.

That knowledge was provided by informant Eddie O'Hare to Frank Wilson, who was initially doubtful of the claims. O'Hare was able to provide a list of ten names, however, that matched those on the list of jurors that even Judge Wilkerson hadn't yet been given.

Wilson was worried that all the work done to bring Capone to trial would be wasted but his fears were allayed by Wilkerson, who was apparently unconcerned by the development. On 5th October 1931, the first day of the trial, Judge Wilkerson started proceedings by exchanging his panel of jurors for another at a trial that was due to start that day in another court.

Capone, who had smiled at the jurors as he walked into court with his bodyguards, was visibly taken aback by this turn of events. The 23 charges of tax evasion against him were then outlined in front of the twelve jurors — all men, since female jurors were not allowed in Illinois until 1939.

The Evidence Against Capone

As various witnesses were called, the evidence against Capone slowly mounted. Tax collector Charles W Arndt affirmed that Capone had not filed any tax returns for the years 1924 to 1929 while Cicero citizen Chester Bragg testified that Capone had clearly stated that he was the owner of the Hawthorne Smoke Shop, a Cicero gambling hall.

That occurred during a citizens' raid on the place and the Reverend Henry Hoover, who led the raid, recalled that Capone had threatened the participants. Some of the most damning evidence came from Leslie Shumway, who had been the cashier at the Hawthorne Smoke Shop. He estimated that profits of over $550,000 accrued during the two years he worked there but was reluctant to identify Capone as the owner, although he did confirm he was in charge of the business.

Crucial to the case was Judge Wilkerson allowing the letter from Capone's lawyers to be admitted into evidence. He over-ruled an objection that, in effect, a lawyer could not make a confession on behalf of his client. This followed agent Frank Wilson's description of Lawrence Mattingly delivering the letter and stating that Capone was willing to pay the tax liability arising from the income shown on it.

Lengthy evidence of Capone's spending was presented by US Attorney Johnson and he emphasized the hypocrisy of someone who, while claiming to be a man of the people, spent obscene amounts of money on himself and gave relatively little to others. More crucially, the high levels of spending were evidence of the income that Capone achieved but did not declare to the tax authorities.

Evidence of Capone's lavish spending came from several witnesses. One of these was Parker Henderson Junior, who had acted as Capone's real estate representative. He recalled that he'd shown Capone several properties in Florida, resulting in him buying the mansion on Palm Island. Another witness testified to seeing large amounts of cash at the property.

Similarly, a clerk at the Metropole Hotel in Chicago told how Capone held lavish parties there and booked the most expensive suites. All of this was paid for in cash, in large denomination bills.

Frank Reis, cashier at the Hawthorne Smoke Shop in 1927, reckoned the profits there that year were about $150,000. This money was used to purchase a large number of cashier's cheques, at least one of which bore Al Capone's signature.

Failure of the Defence Case

Once the prosecution had presented its evidence, the defense took only one day to make its case and did not do a very good job. Having failed to object to the ledgers being brought into evidence due to the statute of limitations, it then presented a mistaken defense based on gambling losses.

It depicted Capone as a gambling addict who had lost the money his business had earned. Since gambling losses could only be offset against winnings, however, this didn't excuse him from paying tax on his business income.

The defense case that Capone had lost $327,000 over six years and this matched his taxable income was totally spurious. In summing up, defense attorney Albert Fink denied there was sufficient evidence of Capone's gross income and accused the government of being determined to convict him at all costs. Whilst pleading that the jury should not convict Capone just because he was a bad person, he also tried to depict his good side and said he was not a tax cheat.

In his summing up, prosecutor Jacob Grossman stressed that Capone's lavish spending was obvious evidence of a very large income and that the letter submitted by lawyer Mattingly proved that Capone knew he had committed tax evasion. US Attorney George Jackson claimed the case would establish whether someone could conduct his affairs in such a way that he was above the law.

The Verdict that Ended Capone's Criminal Career

On 17th October 1931, after deliberating for only nine hours, the jury found Al Capone guilty of tax evasion on several counts. Although he was acquitted on most counts and found guilty of only five, these were enough for the judge to hand down a sentence that was far above the normal level for this type of offence.

He was sentenced to eleven years in jail and ordered to pay court costs of $30,000 and $50,000 in fines as well as the $215,000 plus interest he owed in back taxes. This was the harshest sentence ever imposed for tax fraud, one that visibly shocked Capone and his lawyers.

To appeal the conviction, Capone appointed a Washington-based law firm that was expert in tax law. They filed a writ of habeas corpus, stating that the charges were outside the time limit for prosecution due to the Supreme Court having ruled that tax evasion was not classed as fraud. The judge over-ruled the appeal by deducting the time Capone had spent in Miami from the length of time since the offences.

Effect of the Conviction

That was the end of Capone's criminal career. His role within organized crime in Chicago ceased immediately although the organization he had previously headed simply carried on under new leadership. A succession of bosses followed him, chiefly Frank Nitti, Paul Ricca, Tony Accardo and

Sam Giancana from amongst his previous followers.

The level of violence decreased, however, and Capone's successors adopted a lower profile than he had done. With the end of Prohibition in 1933, the extent of the criminal activities naturally diminished. Nevertheless, the levels of gambling, prostitution and various other illegal activities continued pretty much as before.

One perhaps surprising consequence of Capone's conviction was that back tax receipts went up, both from criminals and law-abiding citizens. That year, the value of unpaid tax filings paid doubled to over $1 million compared to the previous year.

Final Days

In May 1932, at the age of 33 and weighing almost 18 stones, Capone arrived at Atlanta US Penitentiary. A medical examination there revealed that the use of cocaine had perforated his septum and he was suffering from withdrawal symptoms as a result of his addiction. He was also diagnosed as having syphilis and gonorrhoea, the results of his time working in brothels, and which would lead to further deterioration in his health.

His mental health was already showing signs of failing and he was seen as a weak personality who could not deal with bullying. He required the protection of cellmate Red Rudinsky, formerly a minor associate of Capone's gang, which drew accusations of special treatment.

This belief of favoritism was borne out by the conditions under which he lived. Despite his delicate mental state, he was able to use his influence to procure special privileges, furnishings and other items that made his life easier.

His cell had a carpet, personal bedding and other expensive furnishings. There was also a radio and Capone and various inmates and guards would converse and listen to favorite programs. Visitors were plentiful, with friends and family members maintaining a residence in a nearby hotel.

The Transfer to Alcatraz

Partly because of this, and also to provide publicity for the newly opened Alcatraz Federal Penitentiary in San Francisco Bay, Capone was moved there in June 1936. Alcatraz was a maximum security prison intended for violent inmates or those with disciplinary issues. Capone did not fall into those categories so the gaining of publicity for the new facility seemed the most logical reason for moving him there.

Soon after arriving at Alcatraz, Capone was stabbed and slightly wounded by another inmate. The assailant was James 'Tex' Lucas, a 22-year old Texan who was serving thirty years in federal prison for auto theft and bank robbery.

He turned out to be a trouble-maker after transferring to Alcatraz from Leavenworth, since he was later involved in a work strike followed by a violent escape attempt in which a prison officer was killed. Lucas received a life sentence for that and a spell in solitary confinement.

The attack on Capone, on 23rd June 1936, was, he alleged, in response to a threat to kill Lucas. He attacked Capone in the shower room, striking him with one half of a pair of scissors and inflicting superficial cuts to his chest and hands. For the offence, Lucas lost his accumulated time for good behavior, a total of 3,600 days.

During his time in Alcatraz, Capone remained a celebrity. There were constant questions from the press regarding his well-being, activities and anything else about him. Even many years after his death, the cell he occupied is one of the main visitor attractions on 'the Rock'.

Capone's syphilis caused the onset of dementia and eroded his mental capacity. The doctors tried to eradicate the syphilis with malaria injections, hoping the induced fever would clear it.

The treatment almost killed Capone and he spent the last twelve months at Alcatraz in the prison hospital in a confused state. On 6th January 1939, he was released and transferred to the Federal Correctional Institution at Terminal Island near Los

Angeles, to serve a twelve-month sentence for the contempt of court conviction.

Release from Prison and Hospital Treatment

Capone was paroled on 16th November 1939 and referred to John Hopkins Hospital in Baltimore for treatment of syphilis-related illnesses. Admission was refused because of who he was and instead he was admitted to the Union Memorial Hospital. There he became one of the first civilian patients to be administered penicillin as treatment for his syphilis, although by now the condition was far too advanced for it to have much effect.

After several weeks of in-patient and out-patient treatment, Capone left Baltimore on 20th March 1940, donating two Japanese weeping cherry trees to the hospital as thanks for the care he had received. He returned to his mansion on Palm Island for the remaining years of his life, passing the time playing cards and fishing. Test conducted in 1946 by his physician and a psychiatrist concluded that he had the mental capacity of a twelve-year old child.

Capone spent his final days being cared for by his wife and brothers. Most of his time was spent wearing pajamas and having conversations with enemies and colleagues who had died years before, some of them on his orders.

He was reportedly paid by the Outfit a salary of $600 a week, which was barely enough to support his family, pay his staff and maintain the property. Wife Mae kept him in isolation during his last years, knowing any loose public statements about his old organization could well cost him his life while violent outburst brought on by his condition would lose him his freedom.

Illness and Death

Capone suffered a stroke on 21st January 1947. Although he began to recover, he then contracted pneumonia and, on 22nd January, suffered a cardiac arrest.

He died three days later at the age of 48 with his family around him and his physician asked if an autopsy could be conducted on his brain and body for the purposes of medical research. This was refused by the family and the body went to the Philbrick

Funeral Home in Miami Beach where it was placed in a $2,000 massive bronze casket.

The body was available for viewing by permitted guests only although two funeral home employees apparently took surreptitious photographs of Al Capone lying in his open coffin. Huge quantities of flowers arrived and the funeral service was held the following Wednesday at St. Patrick's Roman Catholic Church.

Final Resting Place

Capone was buried at Mount Olivet Cemetery in Chicago close to his father and one brother. Three years afterwards, to counter the constant attention and the vandalism of the gravestone, all the family remains were removed to Mount Carmel

Cemetery in Hillside, Illinois. The original monument was left in place in Mount Olivet Cemetery in an unsuccessful attempt to prevent visitors learning of the new location of the remains.

In a strange twist of fate, Capone died only five days after Andrew John Volstead at the age of 86. Volstead was a member of the United States House of Representatives who, while serving as chairman of the House Judiciary Committee, co-authored the National Prohibition Act of 1916 that bears his name. The act enabled the enforcement of Prohibition, with Capone's subsequent criminal career partly based on the evasion of that legislation.

Mae continued to live in the Palm Island mansion for another five years until she was forced to sell it. She died in 1986, aged 89, but not before she had destroyed all her diaries and private papers relating to Al Capone.

The Capone Legacy

Despite Capone's violent career and the brutality of his past, there is an on-going fascination with his life. Many fictitious characters have been modelled on him and the term 'mobster' or 'gangster' invariably conjures up an image of Al Capone.

There have been plenty of books and articles covering his life and some of these have been made into films. The most well-known of these is Eliot Ness's biography 'The Untouchables', which subsequently became a successful TV series and then a major film. As in many cases, however, the facts weren't always faithfully recorded and the roles of individuals are sometimes exaggerated.

In real life, Capone's influence was enough to change the law in order to deal with him. The 1927 Supreme Court ruling that income tax was due on criminal earnings was intended to help the authorities trap criminals and was instrumental in Capone's eventual downfall.

The End of Prohibition

Later on, the end of the Prohibition era in 1933 was brought about because many Americans enjoyed going to a speakeasy and having a drink. Additionally, it was obvious that Prohibition was actually encouraging criminal activity and many gangsters were getting rich through their bootlegging activities.

So maybe Al Capone's greatest legacy is, ironically, that through violence and brutality, he changed the laws of America. In order to stop him and his peers, activities that he'd undertaken illegally were made legal.

Although there are the contrasting images that Capone leaves behind — on the one hand a do-gooder who helped the poor and on the other a mobster who thought nothing of torturing and killing his opponents — many of his relatives have responded to the bad side. Some have changed their names and moved away from Chicago while others have refused to talk about him or have done so only under the cover of anonymity.

Despite his notoriety as a mobster, one of the biggest ironies of all is that Capone spent longer in jail than he did as a leading criminal. His reign as a crime boss ended after six years at the age of 33. He was then to spend the next seven years six months and fifteen days in prison before his eventual release on parole.

Ongoing Fascination with Capone

The fascination with Capone appears to show little sign of slackening, even seventy years after his death. A recent auction in June 2017 saw a diamond studded platinum pocket watch that belonged to him sold for $84,375.

The triangular watch, on a fourteen carat white gold chain, features 23 diamonds in the shape of his initials, surrounded by a further 26 diamonds and another 72 diamonds on the watch face. Also sold at the auction, for $18,750, was a musical composition — 'Humanesque' — written by Capone in pencil while imprisoned in Alcatraz.

In September 2016, a letter from Capone sold for $62,500 at an auction in Massachusetts. Written to his son from his cell in Alcatraz, the letter, according to experts, showed Capone's softer side.

The Chicago History Museum's website still gets 50,000 hits a month on pages about Capone while visitors to Chicago still drive past his old home and visit his grave site, even though the body is no longer there.

However, the city has made little effort to publicize or preserve the sites associated with Capone, not wishing to draw attention to its violent past.

Capone's Palm Island estate sold for $7.4 million in 2014. It is now available for hire to use for private functions or events, so the fascination with Capone still endures.

Made in the USA
Middletown, DE
27 April 2022